My Faith in You...

Jonathan Vold

SIMORGH PRESS

2022

My Faith in You...

Independently published by Simorgh Press,
900 East Northwest Hwy, Mt Prospect, Illinois

ISBN-13: 9798839384682

My Faith in You...

Table of Contents

I believe; help my unbelief! [1]

---

[1] See page 19.

Introductions

Au lecteur...
mon semblable, —mon frère!
[To the reader...my twin, my brother!] [2]

Doubt is a pain too lonely
to know that
faith is his twin brother. [3]

---

[2] Charles Baudelaire, Preface to Les Fleurs du Mal (1867).

[3] Khalil Gibran, Jesus the Son of Man (1928).

i.

A Dedication

Dear Reader,

This book is about faith. It's my own take on faith, of course, though I rely on the insights and support of many others along the way. Their contributions will be acknowledged on the pages ahead, but first I must acknowledge you. This book, you see, is all about you, to you and for you, intended by its title to include you.

You may prefer to resist the conversation and you may not care to turn these pages, but you are living life with me and around me, before and after me. You are why I write and you help me understand what there is to say. You share your different views with me, you challenge my beliefs and you complete my faith.

Two years ago I dedicated my first collection of quotes, My Hope For You, to my children. I did not name you then, but I had you in mind: you my daughter and you my son, you my stepchildren, you the grandchildren I have not yet met and the great grands I may never know. I hoped to reach you with that book. This time I hope, and begin to believe, that these words can reach the greater family around me. As you read or listen, and even if you don't, you are my friends, my community, my world. You are in my world and I am in yours.

I appreciate every one of the sources of the words compiled in this book, but even more I believe that these contributors have also appreciated you, their audience and inspiration, for hearing their musings, for shaping their perceptions, for adding to their hope and causing their faith to grow. You are the reason for their words.

Faith is always more than words can say, but let this book be a start, and may each of these words — completion, appreciation, trust, immersion, commitment, foundation, belief, awareness, acceptance, understanding, assurance and hope — be a part of my faith in you.

ii.

Definition

So, what is faith?

"It's personal," you once told me. "It's my own choice to make. You need to respect that."

That's a good place to start. Faith is a personal, respectable choice. But with all due respect, I believe faith is something more. It can move from personal to social, becoming something to share. It can be about commitment, as choice grows into certainty. And faith can be invitational, as respect turns to recognition. We should praise the faith that is profoundly personal and willful yet never selfish or exclusive.

But this does not really give us a definite understanding of the word or the experience. What exactly is faith?

We could turn to the bible for our answer. According to the book of Hebrews, chapter 11:

Faith is the assurance of things hoped for, the conviction of things not seen.[4]

Or we can consider the word's etymology. The English word faith comes from the Latin *fides*, or *fid*, which means trust or truth. *Fid* is the root of the words affidavit, fidelity, bonafide, confidence and good ol' loyal Fido. *Fid* is also at the root of a broad philosophy of faith called fideism[5], which generally tells us this:

Faith is the means, more than reason or even without reason, by which one finds truth.

---

[4] Anon., Hebrews 11:1 (ca. 64, tr. NRSV, 2021).

[5] Eugenez Menegoz, Reflections on the Gospel of Salvation (1879), first applied fideism as a philosophy while advancing the principle of salvation by faith, regardless of beliefs or creeds. See also Blaise Pascal, Pensees (ca. 1662), describing the conclusion of God's existence as a wager of faith; Søren Kierkegaard, Fear and Trembling (1843), regarding the move from reason to conviction as a leap of faith; and William James, The Will to Believe (1896), disregarding the lack of evidence in the justification of faith.

Here is what the Oxford Dictionary says:

Faith is 1. complete trust or confidence in someone or something; 2. strong belief in God or in the doctrines of a religion, based on spiritual apprehension rather than proof.[6]

Oxford emphasizes trust (the truth of the fideists) and belief (the conviction of the bible) with the words complete and strong. Trust is followed by confidence, a word that literally means firm trust. Oxford also introduces a little word with big purpose: "in." Suddenly faith is not just about someone or something; it involves trusting and believing in that something or someone.

But then Oxford boldly leaps into the "in," effectively naming the "things" of the bible and offering an end to the fideists' means. As we try to make sense of faith itself, Oxford presumes we need examples and experience to define faith, as if to say:

Faith itself cannot be knowable except by the experience of it.

[6] Oxford University Press, Oxford English and American Dictionaries (2020).

Needing example or experience is a common challenge when we try to define big "things": not just faith, but also hope and love, the sun and the wind, or even God.   Immanuel Kant called it *"ding an sich,"* or "a thing in itself," when he first presented the concept: "And we indeed, rightly considering objects of sense as mere appearances, confess thereby that they are based upon a thing in itself, though we know not this thing as it is in itself, but only know its appearances."[7]

C. S. Lewis once spoke about how we use expedients to describe heaven: "They are not the thing itself; they are only the scent of a flower we have not found, the echo of a tune we have not heard, news from a country we have never yet visited."[8] In other words, we can begin to know of something before we fully understand it.

Wallace Stevens wrote a number of poems about *ding an sich*, even titling one poem "Not Ideas About the Thing But the Thing Itself."[9] Eight

---

[7] Immanuel Kant, Prolegomena to any Future Metaphysics (1783, tr. Paul Carus, 1929).

[8] C. S. Lewis, The Weight of Glory (1941).

[9] Wallace Stevens, Not Ideas About the Thing But the Thing Itself (1954).

years earlier, in "Notes Toward a Supreme Fiction," he wrote:

> You must become an ignorant man again
> And see the sun again with an ignorant
>   eye
> And see it clearly in the idea of it.[10]

Many years earlier, in Plato's "Allegory of the Cave," Socrates spoke of a released prisoner, "able to see the sun, and not mere reflections."[11] Of course, one can never look directly at the sun, as Plato's prisoner would learn, and yet the light of the sun may never be fully appreciated until one leaps out of the shadows.

Which brings us back to that bold leap in the dictionary. Oxford turned to belief in God or religious doctrines as a way to help us understand faith. This may not seem helpful for one who does not have these beliefs, and yet having belief is part of what faith is: we turn to someone or something we can't easily define except by example and experience.

---

[10] Wallace Stevens, Notes Toward a Supreme Fiction (1942).

[11] Plato, The Republic (ca. 376 BC, tr. Benjamin Jowett, 1888).

There is a similar kind of turn in the biblical definition: the "things" hoped for and not seen are what faith is drawn to. They are not faith itself, but one begins to have faith by first having hope in unseen things. Notice that Hebrews 11:1 does not say what the things are, though. The rest of the bible is filled with fundamentals about God and religion (and also love and grace and life, for other big word examples), but the first verse of Hebrews 11 seems set on defining faith more conceptually. In fact, if you read the rest of the chapter, it speaks less of the objects of faith and more of another aspect of faith: how it leads people to action and appreciation before the object is reached and even if it is never reached. Verse 8 says: "By faith Abraham obeyed when he was called to set out for a place that he was to receive as an inheritance, and he set out, not knowing where he was going."[12] This is what is sometimes called the "leap of faith": not knowing and setting out anyway.

Søren Kierkegaard is often credited for advancing this "leap of faith" idea. He never actually used the phrase in his publications, but he wrote about "my theory of the leap" in his journals, asking: "Can there be a transition from quantitative qualification to a qualitative one

---

[12] Anon., Hebrews 11:8 (ca. 64, tr. NRSV, 2021).

without a leap? And does not the whole of life rest in that?"[13] This led to *Fear and Trembling*, where Kierkegaard grappled with the faith-centered leap Abraham took when he was called upon to climb a mountain and sacrifice his son Isaac. Abraham could not have understood this directive, but he obeyed and started gathering wood for an altar. He gave this wood to Isaac to carry, and as he made further preparations with fire and a knife his son asked, "Wait. Where is the lamb?" And all Father Abraham could say, without knowing how or when, was that God would provide. In the end, God did provide a lamb, and Isaac was spared.[14]

Everyday faith doesn't have to be that extreme, of course. In fact, it doesn't even have to be seen as a leap. Abraham's example of forward movement and unquestioning commitment was also one of trust and a calmer acceptance. As Mahatma Gandhi once said, "Faith is not something to grasp, it is a state to grow into."[15]

---

[13] Søren Kierkegaard, Journals (ca. 1843, tr. Howard V. Hong and Edna H. Hong, 1967).

[14] Søren Kierkegaard, Fear and Trembling (1843, with reference to Anon., Genesis 22, ca. 950 BC).

[15] Mahatma Gandhi (1932; as cited by Mahadev Desai, Diaries, 1953).

With this, we have one more way to expand our definition. Whether by leaping or by growing:

Faith is experienced by appreciation.

By this perspective, we can seek to understand faith more deliberately: we can take the staircase one step at a time, we can smell the flowers without trampling on them, we can become more aware of the sun without looking directly into it and we can make our way up the mountain before we know where we are going. And we may never grasp all the answers, but we can come to appreciate the truth as it is revealed.

Let's call this a working definition. If we take the elements of faith found in the bible (assurance, hope and belief), in the word's etymology (fides, or trust) and in the dictionary (the concepts of complete and in), if we reflect the need to experience things not seen or proven, and if we make appreciation a part of our understanding:

Faith is the complete and appreciating trust in something or someone, based on belief in things not seen, acceptance of things not proven and assurance of things to come.

And yet I still want to believe that there is more to faith than this.

iii.

Movement

There is a movement to faith, a pulse that allows us to start with the word complete and to keep going beyond, to appreciate not just a seemingly definable faith but an increasingly infinite understanding. Oxford's definition hinted at this movement several times, with the little word "or." "Or" is an amplifier, always allowing for more to say.

"Or" shows the spectrum of a concept: faith does consist of either trust or confidence, it reflects the comprehensive range of trust and confidence and the transitive nature of one to the other; nor is faith limited to either a someone or a something, and it may even prompt us to blend the two: something about someone or someone who stands for something. "Or" seems to present us with choices, but it also serves as a bridge towards certainty and a step to a fuller comprehension. "Or" is at the heart of our questions, but we come to realize that the answer to "A or B?" can be "yes," and "both." Our questions begin the discussion, and "or" keeps showing us that there is more than we are aware of. "Or" reveals that we may not have an immediate or final answer, even as we may have faith that the answer exists.

In his first book, *Either/Or*, Søren Kierkegaard began to consider how we exist in three spheres: the aesthetic (also called the particular), the ethical (the universal) and the absolute (the complete).[16] *Either/Or* introduced the first two spheres with separate narratives, but neither of these spheres stands forever alone: the particular is inherently part of the universe, and one cannot be ethical without being aesthetic. Later, in *Fear and Trembling*, Kierkegaard focused on the third overlapping sphere of existence: the complete or absolute, which he also called the religious.[17]

Religion, another one of those big words, comes from the Latin *ligare*, to be in league or allegiance with or to be bound to. Think of a liege, the landowner who answered to an overlord in

---

[16] Søren Kierkegaard, Either/Or (1843).

[17] Søren Kierkegaard, Fear and Trembling (1843).

feudal times, or a ligament, the tissue that holds bones together. Religion can be said to reflect the strongest affirmation of faith: there is trust, then the firm trust of confidence, and then the affirmed confidence of a binding relationship.

But the concept of religion is not a requirement, nor is it an initiation. Faith is real in every sphere, either/or, with religion and without. "Or" allows us to move, but it also enables us to choose before we are certain, to have a personal faith before we share it with others. "Or" is a fluid conjunction, at the heart of more, giving us a way to grow from A to B; it is also a permissive word, at the core of before, that does not insist on fixation. "Or" lets us have instances of faithfulness before we experience the moments of an even fuller faith.

There is a compelling trend to this fluidity. The pulse that allows faith to be both complete and appreciating shows up throughout our working definition, repeatedly turning personal to social and choice to certainty. Trust, for instance, is a personal decision, resting in one's own comfort and relying on the path one takes, but then faith rises to confidence. By confiding, *con fides*, we share our trust with someone else.

In the same way, belief, the personal stand one takes on a subject, becomes conviction, which by its root, *con vincere*, means being convinced of something. By its active usage, conviction also means coming to a firm conclusion. With conviction, one proceeds with invincibility; in conclusion, one closes the arguments, convinces others and rests one's case. Conviction, the victory over doubts, makes a believer want to share the belief and lead others to certainty.

Faith also tends to move from something to someone. A child's first faith is in the hands of those who care, the breast that feeds and the ear that hears a cry, but eventually the child comes to know who is behind the hands and the breast and who is listening. The child's universe expands and its faith continues to grow with an increasing appreciation of all that is being provided. This appreciation can be seen in every example of faith: we trust the bridge first, and then the bridgemaker; we trust our tools, and eventually ourselves; we trust the standards we are given, and in time we trust each other. This is how faith moves from instant to moment.

Just for the moment, if you will, consider the personal to social movements within the Christian tradition: One begins with baptism, a personal dedication to a life of faith, then moves, sometimes immediately, to confirmation, making a public affirmation. One starts with a commitment, or giving of oneself, and continues with communion, the celebration of a community. Christians confess their belief with personal acceptance, and then express their faith in a congregational creed. They are shown the spectrum of faith from the personal worship of Mary at Jesus' feet to the social service of her sister Martha in the next room, and yet neither worship nor service are exclusive to being faithful. Finally, Christians consider their faith as both a redemption, being personally saved from sin and death, and a transformation, being born again to a new life.

We can also look outside the church for our examples of faith. One's faith that a bridge will hold him up starts with a dedicated step and continues with confirmation for all to see. One commits to a candidate then joins a community in electing her. One accepts the trustworthiness of a neighbor, then expresses that trust by being part of the neighborhood. One who is devoted to a worthy cause can be quietly supportive or more socially active. And two people who have faith in a relationship can see the redeeming value of no longer living life alone, and they may eventually be transformed to live a life as one.

If we apply the progression that moves us from complete to appreciating throughout each part of our understanding, trust becomes confidence, belief becomes conviction, something becomes someone, the base becomes the strength, and so on, until our working definition is amplified:

Faith is the complete (or infinite) and appreciating (or growing) trust (or confidence) in something (or someone), based on (or affirmed by) belief (or conviction) in things not seen (or apprehended), acceptance (or awareness) of things not proven (or known) and assurance (or certainty) of things to come (or to hope for).

Now we are getting somewhere, but we can go even further. After all, it is said that faith not only moves, but it can move mountains!

iii.

From Movement to Stillness

The challenge of faith moving mountains originated in words of Jesus, first to a father worried about his son's seizures and later to his disciples troubles by their own shortcomings. "If you are able to do anything, help us!" the father said, and Jesus answered, "All things can be done for the one who believes." Immediately the father cried out, "I believe; help my unbelief!" After Jesus cast out the boy's demons, his disciples wondered why they were not able to do the same. "Because of your little faith," Jesus said. "Truly I tell you, if you have faith the size of a mustard seed, you will say to this mountain, 'Move from here to there,' and it will move, and nothing will be impossible for you."[18]

---

[18] Jesus with a father (ca. 33; as cited by Anon., Mark 9:14-29, ca. 70) and with his disciples (Anon., Matthew 17:14-21, ca. 90; both tr. NRSV, 2021).

If it seems impossible to move an obstructive mountain, consider that there may be faith in each small step that digs the tunnel through, grades the road across or hauls aside a truckload of loosened rock. It might be said as well that we move mountains by simply finding the strength and courage to climb them or face them. We can even move mountains by standing still. Think about it: mountains of doubt and frustration and fear, such as the father had, are overcome by appreciation, trust, acceptance, hope and belief. Eventually the father's "if" allows for "will," and belief conquers the unbelief. And that is how a mustard seed can move the earth.

This idea of moving mountains troubled philosopher Friedrich Nietzsche, who once exclaimed, "Faith actually moves no mountains, but instead raises them up where there were none before."[19] Yet Jesus's original use of the metaphor was not at all about faith raising up mountains of obstruction, as Nietzsche argued, but about willfully removing or overcoming the mountains of doubt, argument, resistance and frustration that stand in the way of faith.

––––––––––––––––––––––––––––

[19] Friedrich Nietzsche, The Antichrist (1888, tr. H. L. Mencken, 1920).

It is all about perspective: one can see a mountain as either an obstruction to curse or a challenge to conquer; one can cower in the mountain's shadows or see it as a vantage point; one can see no good in the mountain and walk away from it, as Nietzsche appears to have done, or one can calmly heed the call to walk up the mountain, even as Abraham did with his son.

There is more to Abraham's story. It was after being told he would be the father of many descendants that God suggested he should sacrifice his only son. Walking up that mountain in Moriah had to have been an extreme challenge, and Abraham could have been discouraged, but something made him muster the strength to keep going.[20]

After Abraham came Moses, who led his people through a desert in search of a promised land.[21] You may know Moses for ascending Mount Sinai to get the Ten Commandments, but in his last days, Moses climbed another mountain, Mount Nebo at the outer edge of their destination. There God spoke to him, saying,

---

[20] See Anon., Genesis 17:1-4 and 22:1-18 (ca. 539 BC)).

[21] See Anon., Exodus 13:17-18 (ca. 539 BC), and Anon., Numbers 14:33 (ca. 539 BC).

"This is the land of which I swore to Abraham, to Isaac, and to Jacob, saying, 'I will give it to your descendants'; I have let you see it with your eyes, but you shall not cross over there." Indeed, Moses died on the far side of the river, but "his sight was unimpaired and his vigor had not abated."[22]

Martin Luther King, Jr., who led people across bridges in the battle for civil rights, once stood on a balcony in Memphis, sensing that his movement soon would be limited. Like Moses before him, he would not reach his destination, but on the eve of his assassination he declared famously: "I have been to the mountaintop. ...And I've seen the promised land."[23]

David Brooks, in "The Second Mountain," follows life's journey from a mountain of personal ambition to another mountain that looks beyond oneself. "Moral formation is not individual; it is relational. Character is not something you build sitting in a room thinking about the difference between right and wrong and about your own willpower. Character

---

[22] Anon., Deuteronomy 34:1-8 (ca. 539 BC, tr. NRSV, 2021).

[23] Martin Luther King Jr., Speech in Memphis (1968).

emerges from our commitments. ...When your life is defined by fervent commitments, you are on the second mountain."[24]

There is movement in each of these journeys from one mountain to another, but there is also a certain peace as each of these mountaineers comes to a place where faith, and life, are defined. We can see that peace in Abraham's assent up Moriah, Moses's forty year trek through a desert, Martin's leading others across bridges, and also in the father of the sick son overcoming "if." Faith, it turns out, is not about raising mountains up but rather having the resolve to climb them, learning to proceed with grace and finding peace at the top of the mountain. Movement may be part of how faith overcomes fear and doubt and frustration, but so, after all, is an appreciative stillness.

Stillness is in the personal embrace of what we believe and the willful decision to stand where we are; it's in the sanctity of the respectable faith, and it's in the peace of the moment that serves to calm us, anchor us and keep us in our place. In stillness, the one who stands will still have a pulse, but one can stand with conviction, as Martin Luther did at the onset of his

---

[24] David Brooks, The Second Mountain (2019).

reformation movement.[25] One can stand to cultivate strength, as martial artists do in the stand-still practice of Zhan Zhuang.[26] One can find the strength within, as Hermann Hesse's Siddhartha did in his lifelong search for peace: "Within you, there is a stillness and a sanctuary to which you can retreat at anytime and be yourself."[27] Or (there is always more!) one can find serenity in the stretch of a horizon or at the top of a mountain, catching one's breath at all there is to see.

---

[25] Luther's reformation began in earnest when he refused to retract statements against the papacy when summoned to the Diet of Worms in 1521. In his defense he gave a speech that is said to have ended with the declaration "Here I stand." Official transcripts of his speech did not end with this phrase, but in favor of attributing these words to Luther, it has been noted that he delivered his speech twice, first in Latin and then in German; there was at least some impromptu dialogue after the speech; and early collections of Luther's works, compiled during his life and purportedly under his supervision, included this phrase. See Concordia Publishing House, Did Luther really say, "Here I stand"? (2016).

[26] Literally "standing like a post," a term coined by Wang Xiangzhai (ca. 1963; as cited by Wikipedia: Zhan Zhuang, 2022).

[27] Hermann Hesse, Siddhartha (1922, tr. H. Rossner, 1970).

iv.

The Better Part

So which is better, the movement or the stillness of faith?

Consider the bible story of Mary and Martha: Mary is sitting at Jesus's side while Martha is busy in the kitchen. When the serving sister complains that she is doing all the work, Jesus answers her, "Martha, Martha, you are worried and distracted by many things, but few things are needed—indeed only one. Mary has chosen the better part, which will not be taken away from her."[28]

Was Jesus saying that Mary's faith, full of stillness, was better than Martha's, full of activity? Is stillness the better part? "Better" can

---

[28] Jesus (ca. 33; as cited by Anon., Luke 10:41-42, ca. 120, tr. NRSV, 2021).

be a comparative word, as Martha may have thought, but it does not work as an argument here. It is, instead, an encouraging word of commendation and a call for improvement. Martha, speaking from one room and looking into another, did not succeed at comparing faiths, but Jesus, speaking to both Mary and Martha, effectively succeeded at both commending Mary's faith at the moment and helping Martha understand what it means to be faithful. "Better," for Mary, was a positive approval; "better," for Martha, was an invitation to something more.

This also shows us a better way to look at faith. As we try to define faith, we should strive to have a better perspective, not to be superior over what others know or where they want to be but to have an improved understanding for ourselves and one another; not to critically compare one faith to another but to appreciate what faith means in every instance. At the same time, we should not leave Martha in the other room, as if faith were only personal and never social, or as if Mary's place of worship were a better choice than Martha's acts of service. We are told that Mary chose the better part, and that it was all she needed, but we need to read this carefully.

Mary was not praised for making a choice but rather for having made it with certainty, for attending to one thing instead of many things. The better part was not Mary choosing how to spend her personal time, but rather Mary keeping her focus without distraction. The needful thing was not the process of her choice but the certainty of her faith.

Notice, too, that while both sisters were in different rooms, only Mary was fully in her room and in her faith. But it could just as easily have been reversed, with Mary complaining about Martha being in the other room, Martha being purposefully focused and devoted to her work and Jesus calling Mary out for being distracted and worried and losing sight of what mattered: not the choice before or the worry after but the certainty within.

Mary was content in one room, while Martha, who could have been content in her own room, was distracted and not really into what she was doing. The better part of faith, then, is not about worrying about the faiths of others but being content and at peace in the room you're in.

In our search for the meaning of faith we ought to underscore that little word "in." "In" is the only one of our working definition words that does not have an implicit "or" and does not seem to need to progress to something more. When you're in, you're in.

My brother once sent me something he wrote that included the word "immanence." "I think you meant "imminence," I wrote back, unaware of the word he was teaching me. I had a lot to learn. Imminence, with two *i*'s, concerns the before with an awareness of the after, but immanence with an *a* is all about remaining within the moment, or being "in."

With "in," we have an intriguing preposition that attaches each instance of faith to someone or something. "In" is not a place or a destination, but it suggests one: if I have faith in you, you are where I have placed my trust; if you have faith in a certain future, that is where you want the stairway to lead. At the same time, "in" transcends the destination: when you act in faith, that faith is acting in you, even before you reach the destination. "In," before and after the where is reached, is timeless, without a start or an end. "In" is the first word of the bible, and it makes the first sentence an existential paradox: "In the beginning, God created..."[29] "In," when it is positive, presents a sanctuary: the heart, good

---

[29] Anon., Genesis 1:1 (ca. 539 BC, tr. NRSV, 1989; translation later updated as "When God began to create," NRSV, 2021).

hands, a home, a family, a country; and even when it is something other than positive, it is, for that moment, all there is. "In" is decidedly definitive, without a gray area: you're either in or you're not. "In" transcends the transitive: movement toward is progressive and directional, but movement within is part of a constant pulse. "In," involving immanence, is fundamental to being inherent, indigenous, innate, integral, intrinsical, inevitably inclusive. "In" is, intuitively, complete: one may believe something or someone momentarily, but one believes in something or someone completely. Indeed, this is what it means to be complete: one can be faithful, full of faith, without knowing what that faith means or leads to.

Faith is not a requirement at the "in" door, but rather what leads us to the door, even more than reason.[30] In faith we begin to hold a personal belief or choose a particular direction, even before we are fully conscious of what we believe or choose. We are continually moved from the personal to the social, the aesthetic to the ethical, yet even without reaching the ethical and social we can experience the completeness of trust, hope and belief in whatever our faith is in.

---

[30] See Sanai, Walled Garden of Truth (ca. 1141, tr. David Pendlebury, 1974): "Reason took us as far as the door; but it was his presence that let us in."

We started this journey with a passage from Hebrews 11, but let's read further: after that first verse definition of faith, the writer of Hebrews repeats the phrase "by faith" 19 times, with 19 examples of the thing itself.[31] "By" is a more observational preposition, showing us from the outside what it means to be in.

By the way, with all these bible passages, you may be wondering if I am trying to pull you in to my own room of faith. Perhaps I am. Maybe, in the confidence and conviction of my faith, I cannot help myself from doing so. As Martin Luther said without apology, "Here I stand."[32] But I also hope you will be secure in the rooms you find yourselves in, that you will choose the better part of faith that cannot be taken away from you, and that you will let the activity, the life and the ways of faith in the rooms around you be not a distraction but an encouragement.

I hope you will consider all of these words as encouragement. But I've said enough. In the pages ahead, let's listen to the words of others as they speak to us about the building blocks of faith.

---

[31] Anon., Hebrews 11:8 (ca. 64, tr. NRSV, 2021).

[32] Martin Luther, speech at Worms (1521; see note 26).

Dear reader, I hope you will appreciate what I share with you, as I am grateful for what you give to me. Let's be, one way or another, persons of faith. Let's have faith to move mountains, faith with heartfelt certainty, faith in tomorrow, faith in one another, faith to stand in the presence and faith to leap out of the shadows. Keep that faith and pass it on!

With love and hope, Jonathan.

Faith is the complete and appreciating trust in something or someone, based on belief in things not seen, acceptance of things not proven and assurance of things to come. [33]

---

[33] See Pages 12 and 18.

Reflections of Faith

*When the complete comes,
the partial will come to an end.*

— Paul the Apostle [34]

---

[34] See page 38.

1.

Completion

Faith is complete and absolute. It is the "full" of truthful and hopeful, the "all in" of acceptance and commitment, the certainty of believing and being spiritually aware. Faith is how understanding and standing firm fulfills us.

- God has not called me to be successful.
He has called me to be faithful.

  Mother Teresa (1981; as cited by Senator Mark Hatfield in an interview with Phyllis Theroux, Washington Post, 1981).

- Always aim at complete harmony of thought and word and deed. Always aim at purifying your thoughts and everything will be well.

  Mahatma Gandhi, Harijan (1937).

- When we consider what is our thought of God we find that it is our own soul stripped of all inferiority and carried out to perfection.

  Ralph Waldo Emerson, Sermon 86 (ca. 1830, as published by Teresa Toulouse and Albert J. Von Frank, The Complete Sermons of Ralph Waldo Emerson, Volume 2, 1990).

- The idea of God, sublime and awful as it is, is the idea of our own spiritual nature, purified and enlarged to infinity.

  William Ellery Channing, Likeness of God (1828).

- There is no repose for the mind except in the absolute; for feeling except in the infinite; for the soul except in the divine.

  Henri-Frédéric Amiel, The Journal Intime (1882, tr. Mary Augusta Ward, 1885).

- Eventually, all things merge into one, and a river runs through it.

    Norman Maclean, A River Runs Through It (1976).

- I'm not going to put my ultimate faith in the little gods that can be destroyed in an atomic age, but the God who has been our help in ages past, and our hope for years to come, and our shelter in the time of storm, and our eternal home. That's the God that I'm putting my ultimate faith in. That's the God that I call upon you to worship this morning. Go out and be assured that that God is going to last forever. Storms might come and go. Our great skyscraping buildings will come and go. Our beautiful automobiles will come and go, but God will be here. Plants may wither, the flowers may fade away, but the word of our God shall stand forever and nothing can ever stop him. All of the P-38s in the world can never reach God. All of our atomic bombs can never reach him. The God that I'm talking about this morning is the God of the universe and the God that will last through the ages.

    Martin Luther King Jr., Rediscovering Lost Values (1954).

- For we know only in part, and we prophesy only in part; but when the complete comes, the partial will come to an end. ...For now we see only a reflection, as in a mirror, but then we will see face to face. Now I know only in part; then I will know fully, even as I have been fully known.

  Paul the Apostle, 1 Corinthians 13: 9, 12 (ca. 54, tr. NRSV, 2021).

- ...Progress is man's distinctive mark
    alone.
  Not God's, and not the beast's; God is,
    they are;
  Man partly is and wholly hopes to be.

  Robert Browning, A Death in the Desert (1864).

- God has not the slightest difficulty in bringing to a fullness of creation the person who is in some way incomplete and recognizes this. The problem is with those who think that they are complete, and that creation is, at least in their case, finished.

  James Alison, Faith Beyond Resentment (2001).

- The Sea
  Will be the Sea
  Whatever the drop's philosophy.
  Attar of Nishapur (ca. 1221, as cited by Lynn Plourde, Dad, Aren't You Glad?, 1974).

- There is only one religion, though there are a hundred versions of it.
  George Bernard Shaw, Preface to Plays Pleasant and Unpleasant, Vol. II (1898).

- In reality there are as many religions as there are individuals.
  Mahatma Gandhi, Indian Home Rule (1909, tr. Mahatma Gandhi, 1910).

- Every truth—if it really is truth—presents itself as universal, even if it is not the whole truth. If something is true, then it must be true for all people and at all times. Beyond this universality, however, people seek an absolute which might give to all their searching a meaning and an answer—something ultimate, which might serve as the ground of all things. In other words, they seek a final explanation, a supreme value, which refers to nothing beyond itself and which puts an end to all questioning.
  Pope John Paul II, Faith and Reason (1998, tr. Vatican Publishing House).

- The discovery of the T.O.E. [theory of everything]—the ultimate explanation of the universe at its most microscopic level, a theory that does not rely on any deeper explanation—would provide the firmest foundation on which to build our understanding of the world. Its discovery would mark the beginning, not the end.

  Brian Greene, The Elegant Universe (1999).

- Begin whatever you have to do: the beginning of a work stands for the whole.

  Ausonius, Inconnexa (ca. 395; as cited by Kate Louise Roberts, Hoyt's New Cyclopedia of Practical Quotations, 1922).

- Thy faith hath made thee whole.

  Jesus (ca. 33; as cited by Anon., Luke 17:19, ca. 120, tr. KJV, 1611; alternatively translated as "your faith has made you well," NRSV, 2021).

- *JERRY MAGUIRE* [as played by Tom Cruise] You complete me.

  Cameron Crowe, Jerry Maguire (1996).

- As the picture in the mind of the painter, as the poem in the mind of the poet, so was all creation in the mind of God from all eternity, in uncreated simplicity.

  William Ralph Inge, Light, Life, and Love (1904).

My faith in you... adds to all that I believe. You complete me through demonstration and affirmation, teaching and shaping. You show me who I am by all that you are, and you make me want to be part of the all.

Strive for the greater gifts. And I will show you a still more excellent way.

— Paul the Apostle [35]

---

[35] See page 47.

2.

Appreciation

Faith is completeness and beyond, with an affinity for infinity. Faith moves from personal to social and grows as it goes, yet it is everything at every moment, allowing us to appreciate where we are as much as where we are going.

- *BUZZ LIGHTYEAR* [as played by Tom Hanks]
  To infinity, and beyond!
    Joss Whedon, Andrew Stanton, Joel Cohen and Alec Sokolow, Toy Story (1995).

- Nothing infinite can have a boundary.
    Thomas Aquinas, Summa Theologica (ca. 1270, tr. Fathers of the English Dominican Province, 1920).

- A narrow religion, a sectarian religion, an exclusive religion can live only for a limited time and a limited purpose.
    Sri Aurobindo, Uttarpara Speech (1909).

- The idea of infinity cannot be expressed in words or even described.... The absolute is only attainable through faith and in the creative act.
    Andrei Tarkovsky, Sculpting in Time (1986).

- To accomplish great things we must not only act, but also dream; not only plan, but also believe.
    Anatole France, Introductory speech before the French Academy (1896; as cited by Thomas Juli, Leadership Principles for Project Success, 2010).

- You can only apprehend the Infinite by a faculty that is superior to reason.
    Plotinus (ca. 260; as cited by Robert A. Voughan, Hours of the Mystics, 1856).

- There are times in the history of men and nations, when they stand so near the vail that separates mortals from the immortals, time from eternity, and men from their God, that they can almost hear the beatings, and feel the pulsations, of the heart of the Infinite.

  James A. Garfield, Congressional speech on the first anniversary of Lincoln's death (1866).

- You have first an instinct, then an opinion, then a knowledge, as the plant has root, bud, and fruit. Trust the instinct to the end, though you can render no reason. It is vain to hurry it. By trusting it to the end it shall ripen into truth, and you shall know why you believe.

  Ralph Waldo Emerson, Intellect (1841).

- Growth is just awareness of more and more.

  Elizabeth Goudge, The Scent of Water (1963).

- Growth is the only evidence of life.

  John Henry Newman, Apologia pro Vita Sua (1864).

- Faith is not something to grasp, it is a state to grow into.

  Mahatma Gandhi (1932; as cited by Mahadev Desai, Diaries (1953).

- For, after all, you do grow up, you do outgrow your ideals, which turn to dust and ashes, which are shattered into fragments ; and if you have no other life, you just have to build one up out of these fragments.

  Fyodor Dostoevsky, White Nights (1848, tr. David Magarshack, 2001).

- "We fight not for ourselves but for growth – growth that goes on forever. Tomorrow, whether we live or die, growth will conquer through us. That is the law of the spirit forevermore. To grow according to the will of God! To grow out of these cracks and crannies, out of these shadows and darknesses, into greatness and the light! Greater," he said, speaking with slow deliberation, "greater, my Brothers! And then – still greater. To grow and again – to grow. To grow at last into the fellowship and understanding of God."

  H. G. Wells, The Food of the Gods and How It Came to Earth (1904).

- Strive for perfection in everything we do. Take the best that exists and make it better.

  Frederick Henry Royce (ca. 1933; as cited by Francis J. Gouillart, Transforming the Organization, 1996).

- But strive for the greater gifts. And I will show you a still more excellent way.
  Paul the Apostle, 1 Corinthians 12:31 (ca. 54, tr. NRSV, 2021).

- Excellence is the gradual result of always striving to do better.
  Pat Riley (ca. 2015; as cited by John C. Maxwell, The Leadership Handbook, 2015).

- Next to excellence is the appreciation of it.
  William Makepeace Thackeray (ca. 1863; as cited by Edward Day, Collacon: An Encyclopaedia of Prose Quotations, 1884).

- Appreciation is a wonderful thing: It makes what is excellent in others belong to us as well.
  Voltaire (ca. 1778; as cited by Evan Esar, 20,000 Quips and Quotes, 1968).

- The good of man is a working of the soul in the way of excellence in a complete life... for as it is not one swallow or one fine day that makes a spring, so it is not one day or a short time that makes a man blessed and happy.
  Aristotle, Niomachean Ethics (ca. 350 BCE, as paraphrased by Will Durant, The Story of Philosophy, 1926).

- We are what we repeatedly do. Excellence, then, is not an act but a habit.
  Will Durant, The Story of Philosophy (1926).

- Excellence is a process that should occupy all our days.
  Ted Engstrom, The Pursuit of Excellence (1982).

- The steadfast love of the Lord never
  ceases,
  his mercies never come to an end;
  they are new every morning;
  great is your faithfulness.
  Jeremiah, Lamentations 3:22-23 (ca. 570 BC, tr. NRSV, 2021).

- Great is Thy faithfulness, Great is Thy Faithfulness. Morning by morning new mercies I see.
  Thomas Chisholm, Great Is Thy Faithfulness (1923).

- The Biblical words about the genesis of heaven and earth are not words of information but words of appreciation. The story of creation is not a description of how the world came into being but a song about the glory of the world's having come into being.
  Abraham Joshua Heschel, Who Is Man? (1965).

My faith in you... appreciates you, for who you are and also for who you can be. As I love to learn and learn to love you, I pray each today is excellent, each tomorrow even better.

The spirit enters into me
and I submit to trust.

— *Peter Gabriel* [36]

---

[36] See page 56.

3.

Trust

Faith is trust turning to confidence: one has trust within and then one proceeds with confidence and brings it to others as truth to be shared. Faith is the trust of the lamb to the shepherd, the truth of the sheep to the flock. In trust, we hold what is true and stand by what we believe.

- At this point I have one certain test. Mankind are not held together by lies. Trust is the foundation of society. Where there is no truth, there can be no trust, and where there is no trust, there can be no society. Where there is society, there is trust, and where there is trust, there is something upon which it is supported.
  Frederick Douglass, Our Composite Nationality (1869).

- And you will know the truth, and the truth will make you free.
  Jesus (ca. 33; as cited by Anon., John 8:32, ca. 100, tr. NRSV, 2021).

- All I want is the truth.
  John Lennon, Gimme Some Truth (1971).

- You have to trust that the dots will somehow connect in your future. You have to trust in something — your gut, destiny, life, karma, whatever. This approach has never let me down, and it has made all the difference in my life.
  Steve Jobs, Address at Stanford University (2005).

- Love...rejoices in the truth.
  Paul the Apostle, 1 Corinthians 13:5-7 (ca. 54, tr. NRSV, 2021).

- All the breath and the bloom of the year
       in the bag of one bee:
  All the wonder and wealth of the mine
       in the heart of one gem:
  In the core of one pearl all the shade
       and the shine of the sea:
  Breath and bloom, shade and shine, —
       wonder, wealth, and —
       how far above them —
  Truth, that's brighter than gem,
  Trust, that's purer than pearl, —
  Brightest truth, purest trust
       in the universe, —
       all were for me
  In the kiss of one girl.

  Robert Browning, Summum Bonum (1889).

- For truth has such a face and such
       a mien,
  As to be lov'd needs only to be seen.

  *John Dryden, The Hind and the Panther
  (1687).*

- They who know the truth are not equal to
  those who love it, and they who love it
  are not equal to those who delight in it.

  *Confucius (ca. 479 BC; as cited by Anon., The
  Confucian Analects, ca. 140 BC, tr. James
  Legge, 1861).*

- What matter that the man stands for much I cannot love—the moment he touches the realms of truth he enters my world and is my friend.

  John Lancaster Spalding, Aphorisms and Reflections (1901).

- It takes two to speak the truth — one to speak, and another to hear.

  Henry David Thoreau, A Week on the Concord and Merrimack Rivers (1849).

- Plato is my friend — Aristotle is my friend — but my greatest friend is truth.

  Isaac Newton, Certain Philosophical Questions (1664).

- Trust men, and they will be true to you; treat them greatly, and they will show themselves great.

  Ralph Waldo Emerson, Prudence (1841).

- Man has had to fight for every atom of the truth, and has had to pay for it almost everything that the heart, that human love, that human trust cling to. Greatness of soul is needed for this business: the service of truth is the hardest of all services.

  Friedrich Nietzsche, The Antichrist (1895, tr. H. L. Mencken, 1923).

- God has placed in the human heart a desire to know the truth—in a word, to know himself—so that, by knowing and loving God, men and women may also come to the fullness of truth about themselves.

  Pope John Paul II, Faith and Reason (1998, tr. Vatican Publishing House).

- All I have seen teaches me to trust the Creator for all I have not seen.

  Ralph Waldo Emerson, Immortality (1861).

- For we cannot do anything against the truth but only for the truth.

  Paul the Apostle, 2 Corinthians 13:8 (ca. 56, tr. NRSV, 2021).

- Truth can never be told so as to be understood, and not be believed.

  William Blake, The Marriage of Heaven and Hell (1790)

- A honest man's word is as good as his bond.

  Miguel de Cervantes, Don Quixote (1615, tr. P. A. Motteux, 1879).

- Trust yourself. You know more than you think you do.

  Benjamin Spock, Baby and Child Care (1977).

- *POLONIUS*
  To thine own self be true,
  And it must follow, as the night the day,
  Thou canst not then be false to any man.
    William Shakespeare, Hamlet, Act I, Scene 3 (1609).

- Trust to me!
  Oh, if in this hour I endeavor
  To trace the shade creeping across the
      young life
  Which, in prayer till this hour, I have
      watch'd through its strife
  With the shadow of death, 'tis with this
      faith alone,
  That, in tracing the shade, I shall find
      out the sun.
  Trust to me!
    Owen Meredith, Lucile (1860).

- Blessed are those who trust in the Lord,
  whose trust is the Lord.
    Jeremiah, Jeremiah 17:7 (ca. 550 BC, tr. NRSV, 2021).

- The spirit enters into me
  And I submit to trust.
    Peter Gabriel, The Rhythm of the Heat (1982).

My faith in you... is trusting you as you walk with me, sharing a future we cannot see and believing that what is true for you is also true for me.

In the beginning, God....
— *Anonymous* [37]

---

[37] See page 60.

4.

Immersion

Faith is all in. It leaps beyond reservation, not just trusting but trusting in, not merely confiding but having confidence in. The immersion, inclusion and immanence of faith gives the believer a place to be, a creed to carry, a life to live and a walk to walk.

- In the beginning, God created...
  > *Anon., Genesis 1:1 (ca. 539 BC, tr. KJV, 1611; see also note 29 on p. 28).*

- The only joy in the world is to begin. It is good to be alive because living is beginning, always, every moment.
  > *Cesare Pavese, This Business of Living: Diaries 1935-1950 (1952, tr. A. E. Murch).*

- The first step, my son, which one makes in the world, is the one on which depends the rest of our days.
  > *Voltaire, L'Indiscret (1725, tr. Hoyt's New Cyclopedia of Practical Quotations, 1922).*

- What if, rather than speaking or dreaming of an absolute beginning, we speak of a leap?
  > *Søren Kierkegaard, Concluding Unscientific Postscript to Philosophical Fragments (1846, tr. Howard V. Hong and Edna H. Hong, 1985).*

- Fear looks; faith jumps.
  > *Smith Wigglesworth (ca. 1947; as cited by Albert Hibbert, Smith Wigglesworth, The Secret of His Power, 2007).*

- That's one small step for a man, one giant leap for mankind.
  > *Neil Armstrong, Flight Transcript of Apollo 11 (1969).*

- And take risk. NASA has this phrase that they like, "Failure is not an option." But failure has to be an option. In art and exploration, failure has to be an option. Because it is a leap of faith. And no important endeavor that required innovation was done without risk. You have to be willing to take those risks. ... In whatever you are doing, failure is an option. But fear is not.

  James Cameron, Before Avatar ...a curious boy (2010, ted.com).

- Atheism ...tries to use reason to demolish a structure that is not built upon reason; because, though rational argument may take us to the edge of belief, we require a "leap of faith" to jump the chasm.

  Sydney J. Harris, Pieces of Eight (1982).

- Theirs not to make reply,
  Theirs not to reason why,
  Theirs but to do and die.

  Alfred, Lord Tennyson, The Charge of the Light Brigade 1854).

- Let us Do or Die!

  Robert Burns, Robert Bruce's March to Bannockburn (1793).

- Leap! leap up, and lick the sky! I leap with thee; I burn with thee; would fain be welded with thee; defyingly I worship thee!

  Herman Melville, Moby Dick (1851).

- Our faith, our knowledge that God is in charge, must make us ready to take risks, to be venturesome and innovative; yes, to dare to walk where angels might fear to tread.

  Desmond Tutu, God is Clearly Not a Christian: Pleas for Interfaith Tolerance (2011).

- It is terribly important to realize that the leap of faith is not so much a leap of thought as of action. For while in many matters it is first we must see then we will act; in matters of faith it is first we must do then we will know, first we will be and then we will see. One must, in short, dare to act wholeheartedly without absolute certainty.

  William Sloane Coffin, Credo (2004).

- The problem inherent in the surface of things, and only in the surface of things, is the heart of things.

  Leo Strauss, Thoughts on Machiavelli (1958).

- Religion and science have always been matters of faith in something. It is the same something.

  Gene Wolfe, The Book of the New Sun: The Citadel of the Autarch (1983).

- Believe in something, even if it means sacrificing everything.

  Colin Kaepernick, Nike Ad Campaign (2018).

- *GOD [as played by George Burns]*
  If you find it hard to believe in me, maybe it would help you to know that I believe in you.

  Larry Gelbart, Oh, God! (1977).

- The greatest source of grit I know, the force that allows us to overcome every failure, every setback, every defeat, and keep going and growing, is faith in God's faith in us.

  Jonathan Sacks, Strength from Faith Is God's Faith in Us (2012).

- Reason took us as far as the door, but it was grace that let us in.

  Sanai, Walled Garden of Truth (ca. 1141, tr. David Pendlebury, 1974).

- The Son himself will also be subjected to the one who put all things in subjection under him, so that God may be all in all.

  Paul the Apostle, 1 Corinthians 15: 28 (ca. 54, tr. NRSV, 2021).

- All things in this creation exist within you, and all things in you exist in creation; there is no border between you and the closest things, and there is no distinction between you and the farthest things, and all things, from the lowest to the loftiest, from the smallest to the greatest, are within you as equal things. In one atom are found all of the elements of the earth; in one motion of the mind are found all the motions of all the laws of existence; in one drop of water are found the secrets of all the endless oceans; in one aspect of you are found all the aspects of existence.

  Kahlil Gibran, Iram, City of Lofty Pillars (1921, tr. A.R. Ferris, 1947).

- You must not lose faith in humanity. Humanity is an ocean; if a few drops of the ocean are dirty, the ocean does not become dirty.

  Mahatma Gandhi (ca. 1948; as cited by Louis Fischer, Gandhi: His Life and Message for the World (1954).

My faith in you... is insistent, immanent, inherent, innate, indigenous, integral, intrinsical and inevitably inclusive: I walk with you, live for you, think of you and believe in you.

Willing is not enough, we must do.
— *Johann Wolfgang von Goethe* [38]

---

[38] See page 69.

5.

Commitment

Faith has purpose and direction. It commits to turning towards something and goes beyond being and believing to maintaining the belief and acting upon it. Faith not only has something to believe in and someone to trust, faith has a reason to serve, a cause to belong to and a call to heed.

- You're gonna have to serve somebody.
  Bob Dylan, Gotta Serve Somebody (1979).

- Whoever wishes to be great among you must be your servant, and whoever wishes to be first among you must be slave of all. For the Son of Man came not to be served but to serve and to give his life as a ransom for many.
  Jesus (ca. 33; as cited by Anon., Mark 10: 43-45, ca. 70, tr. NRSV, 2021).

- Commitment is an act, not a word.
  Jean-Paul Sartre, interview with John Gerassi (1971, New York Times Magazine).

- The essence of faith is fewness of words and abundance of deeds.
  Bahá'u'lláh, Words of Wisdom (ca. 1892, tr. Shoghi Effendi, 1923).

- Faith by itself, if it has no works, is dead.
  James the Just, James 2:17 (ca. 69, tr. NRSV, 2021).

- He must trust, and he must have faith. And so he builds, because what is building, and rebuilding and rebuilding again, but an act of faith?
  Dave Eggers, Zeitoun (2009).

- Faith is not just something you have, it's something you do.

  Barrack Obama, Speech at Global Summit on AIDS and the Church (2006).

- Knowledge is not enough, we have to apply it; wanting is not enough, there has to be action.

  Johann Wolfgang von Goethe, Wilhelm Meister's Journeyman Years (1829, tr. Elisabeth Stopp, 1998; variant translation on p. 66 as cited by Banker's Monthly, 1960, tr. unknown).

- A man who had two sons ... went to the first and said, "Son, go out and work in my vineyard today." But he answered and said, "I will not," but afterward he repented of it and he went. And the father went to the second and said the same. But he answered, "I will, sir," and he did not go. Which of the two did the will of his father?

  Søren Kierkegaard, Works of Love (1847, tr. Howard V. Hong and Edna H. Hong, 1995).

- I would rather work with five people who really believe in what they are doing rather than five hundred who can't see the point.

  Patrick Dixon, Building a Better Business (2005).

- *JULIAN ASSANGE [as played by Benedict Cumberbatch]*
  It takes two things to change the world, and you'd be surprised how many people have good ideas, but— commitment? true commitment?—that's the hard one.   It requires sacrifice.
  Josh Singer, The Fifth Estate (2013).

- I call that mind free, ...which does not content itself with a passive or hereditary faith, which opens itself to light whencesoever it may come, which receives new truth as an angel from heaven.
  William Ellery Channing, Spiritual Freedom (1830)

- All the beautiful sentiments in the world weigh less than a single lovely action.
  James Russell Lowell, Rousseau and the Sentimentalists (1867).

- Existence was given us for action, rather than indolent and aimless contemplation; our worth is determined by the good deeds we do, rather than by the fine emotions we feel. They greatly mistake, who suppose that God cares for no other pursuit than devotion.
  Elias Lyman Magoon, Proverbs for the People (1849).

- The belief that God will do everything for man is as untenable as the belief that man can do everything for himself. It, too, is based on a lack of faith. We must learn that to trust God with the expectation that he will do everything while we do nothing, is not faith, but superstition.

  Martin Luther King Jr., Strength to Love: The Answer to a Perplexing Question (1963).

- For, had God so willed, He could surely have made you all one single community; however, He lets go astray him that wills [to go astray], and guides aright him that wills [to be guided]; and you will surely be called to account for all that you ever did!

  Muhammad, Quran 16:93 (ca. 632, tr. Muhammad Asad, with bracketed clauses added by Asad, 1980).

- A man who waits to believe in action before acting is anything you like, but he's not a man of action. It is as if a tennis player before returning a ball stopped to think about his views of the physical and mental advantages of tennis. You must act as you breathe.

  Georges Clemenceau, Clemenceau, The Events of His Life as Told by Himself to His Former Secretary, Jean Martet (ca. 1929, tr. Milton Waldman, 1930).

- Let each man think himself an act of God,
  His mind a thought, his life a breath of
  God.
  > *Philip James Bailey, Festus: Proem (1845).*

- Pray as if everything depends on God and
  work as if everything depends on you.
  > *Ignatius of Loyola (ca. 1556; as cited by Pedro de Ribadeneira, Life of Loyola, 1572, as recited by Pope John Paul II, Catechism of the Catholic Church, 1992, tr. Vatican Publishing House).*

- Better remain silent, better not even think,
  if you are not prepared to act.
  > *Annie Besant, India's Awakening (1910).*

- Ask not what your country can do for you
  — ask what you can do for your country.
  > *John F. Kennedy, Inaugural address (1961).*

- It is rather for us here dedicated to the
  great task remaining before us, that from
  these honored dead we take increased
  devotion to that cause for which they
  gave the last full measure of devotion.
  > *Abraham Lincoln, Gettysburg Address (1863).*

- All the beautiful sentiments in the world
  weigh less than a single lovely action.
  > *James Russell Lowell, Rosseau and the Sentimentalists (1867.*

My faith in you... is my commitment to you as you go forward, not because I am good at this but because I can see the good in you, all the time, a goodness that makes me want to give you my best.

*The loftiest edifices need
the deepest foundations.*
— George Santayana [39]

---

[39] See page 77.

6.

Foundation

Faith is foundation, firm and strong, the basis for our belief beyond doubt and the support of our reasoning against all resistance.   Faith is the anchor in the storm, more firmly entrenched by the blowing winds. It is the spirit by which we live and the strength by which we stand.

- Faith like Job's cannot be shaken because it is the result of having been shaken.

  Abraham Joshua Heschel (ca. 1972; as cited by Phillip Yancey, Disappointment With God, 1988).

- As concerning faith we ought to be invincible, and more hard, if it might be, than the adamant stone.

  Martin Luther, Commentary on Galatians (1535, tr. Edwinus London, 1575).

- I have fought a good fight; I have finished the race; I have kept the faith.

  Paul the Apostle, 2 Timothy 4:7 (ca. 67, tr. NRSV, 2021).

- The foundations of a person are not in matter but in spirit.

  Ralph Waldo Emerson, Nature (1836).

- We look upon this shaken Earth, and we declare our firm and fixed purpose — the building of a peace with justice in a world where moral law prevails. The building of such a peace is a bold and solemn purpose. To proclaim it is easy. To serve it will be hard.

  Dwight D. Eisenhower, Second Inaugural Address (1957).

- Where the battle rages the loyalty of the soldier is proved; and to be steady on all the battle-field besides is mere flight and disgrace to him if he flinches at that one point.

      Elizabeth Charles, The Chronicles of the Schoenberg Cotta Family (1864).

- The porter runs to the heavy load and takes it from others knowing burdens are the foundations of ease and bitter things the forerunners of pleasure. See the porters struggle over the load! It's the way of those who see the truth of things.

      Rumi, Masnavi II (ca. 1273, tr. Kabir and Camille Helminski, 2011).

- Do you wish to rise? Begin by descending. You plan a tower that will pierce the clouds? Lay first the foundation of humility. It was pride that changed angels into devils; it is humility that makes men as angels.

      Augustine of Hippo (ca. 430; as cited by Thomas of Ireland, Manipulus Florum, 1306).

- The loftiest edifices need the deepest foundations.

      George Santayana, The Life of Reason (1933).

- If you have built castles in the air, your work need not be lost; that is where they should be. Now put the foundations under them.
  Henry David Thoreau, Walden (1854).

- Give me the place to stand, and I shall move the earth.
  Archimedes (ca. 212 BC; as cited by Pappus of Alexandria, Synagoge, 340, tr. Ivor Thomas, 1941).

- Here I stand. I cannot do otherwise.
  Martin Luther, speech at Worms (1521; as cited by Edward Thomas Vaughan, Preface to On the Bondage of the Will, 1823).

- Stand therefore, and belt your waist with truth and put on the breastplate of righteousness and lace up your sandals I preparation for the gospel of peace. With all of these, take the shield of faith, with which you will be able to quench all the flaming arrows of the evil one. Take the helmet of salvation and the sword of the Spirit, which is the word of God.
  Paul the Apostle, Ephesians 6:14-17 (ca. 62, tr. NRSV, 2021).

- Everyone, then, who hears these words of mine and acts on them will be like a wise man who built his house on rock. The rain fell, the floods came, and the winds blew and beat on that house, but it did not fall because it had been founded on rock. And everyone who hears these words of mine and does not act on them will be like a foolish man who built his house on sand. The rain fell, and the floods came, and the winds blew and beat against that house, and it fell—and great was its fall!

  Jesus (ca. 33); as cited by Anon., Matthew 7:24-27 (ca. 90, tr. NRSV, 2021).

- God is our refuge and strength, a very present help in trouble. Therefore we will not fear, though the earth should change, though the mountains shake in the heart of the sea; though its waters roar and foam, though the mountains tremble with its tumult.

  Anon., Psalm 46:1-3 (ca. 701 BC, tr. NRSV, 2021).

- A mighty fortress is our God,
  A bulwark never failing.

  Martin Luther, A Mighty Fortress Is Our God (1529, tr. Frederic Henry Hedge, 1853).

- I decided early to give my life to something eternal and absolute. Not to these little gods that are here today and gone tomorrow, but to God who is the same yesterday, today, and forever. Not in the little gods that can be with us in a few moments of prosperity, but in the God who walks with us through the valley of the shadow of death, and causes us to fear no evil. That's the God. Not in the god that can give us a few Cadillac cars and Buick convertibles, as nice as they are, that are in style today and out of style three years from now, but the God who threw up the stars to bedeck the heavens like swinging lanterns of eternity. Not in the god that can throw up a few skyscraping buildings, but the God who threw up the gigantic mountains, kissing the sky, as if to bathe their peaks in the lofty blues. Not in the god that can give us a few televisions and radios, but the God who threw up that great cosmic light that gets up early in the morning in the eastern horizon, who paints its technicolor across the blue—something that man could never make.

  Martin Luther King Jr., Rediscovering Lost Values (1954).

My faith in you... stands with you and beside you, giving you a steady hold and feeling your support returned. Individually we may waver as the world turns, but together we stand on solid ground.

Believe that life is worth living, and your belief will help create the fact.

— William James [40]

---

[40] See page 84.

7.

Belief

Faith believes beyond doubt. Everyone doubts, but faith faces doubt and recovers from it by discovering truth and embracing it. Doubt forgets what one believes in, but faith remembers it, again and again, constantly believing and rebelieving.

- He who wishes to learn must believe.
  Aristotle, On Sophistical Refutations (350 BC, as cited by Josef Pieper, On Faith, 1962, tr. Richard and Clara Winston, 1963).

- Believe that life is worth living, and your belief will help create the fact.
  William James, Is Life Worth Living? (Speech to the Harvard YMCA, 1895).

- [A father with his sick son, to Jesus:] "If you are able to do anything, help us! have compassion on us!" Jesus said to him, "If you are able! All things can be done for the one who believes." Immediately the father of the child cried out, "I believe; help my unbelief!"
  Jesus and a father with his sick son (ca. 33; as cited by Anon., Mark 9: 22-24, ca. 70, tr. NRSV, 2021).

- Belief consists in accepting the affirmations of the soul; unbelief, in denying them.
  Ralph Waldo Emerson, Montaigne: Or, The Skeptic (1850).

- First doubt your doubts before you doubt your faith.
  Dieter F. Uchtdorf, Come Join With Us (2013).

- We should never believe anything we have not dared to doubt.

  Christina, Queen of Sweden, Maxims of a Queen (ca. 1689, tr. Una Birch, 1907).

- If you can keep your head when all
      about you
  Are losing theirs and blaming it on you,
  If you can trust yourself when all men
      doubt you,
  But make allowance for their doubting
      too...

  Rudyard Kipling, If– (1910).

- There lives more faith in honest doubt,
  Believe me, than in half the creeds.

  Alfred, Lord Tennyson, In Memoriam A.H.H. (1849).

- I can understand myself in believing, although in addition I can in a relative misunderstanding understand the human aspect of this life, but comprehend faith or comprehend Christ, I cannot.

  Søren Kierkegaard, Has a Man the Right to Let Himself Be Put to Death for the Truth? (1847, tr. Howard V. Hong and Edna H. Hong, 1997).

- Peter answered him, "Lord, if it is you, command me to come to you on the water." He said, "Come." So Peter got out of the boat, started walking on the water, and came toward Jesus. But when he noticed the strong wind, he became frightened, and, beginning to sink, he cried out, "Lord, save me!" Jesus immediately reached out his hand and caught him, saying to him, "You of little faith, why did you doubt?"

  Jesus and Peter (ca. 33; as cited by Anon., Matthew 14:28-31, ca. 90, tr. NRSV, 2021).

- Reality is that which, when you stop believing in it, doesn't go away.

  Philip K. Dick, How To Build A Universe That Doesn't Fall Apart Two Days Later (1978).

- Einstein's letters teach us impressively the fact that even an exact science like physics is based on fundamental beliefs.

  Max Born, Natural Philosophy of Cause and Chance (1949).

- I believe in intuitions and inspirations. I sometimes feel that I am right. I do not know that I am.

  Albert Einstein, interview with George Sylvester Viereck (1929, The Saturday Evening Post).

- He that will believe only what he can fully comprehend, must have a very long head, or a very short creed.
  Charles Caleb Colton, Lacon (1820).

- You say I am loved
     when I can't feel a thing
  You say I am strong
     when I think I am weak
  And You say I am held
     when I am falling short
  And when I don't belong, oh,
     You say I am Yours
  And I believe, oh, I believe
     What You say of me
  I believe
  Lauren Daigle, You Say (2018).

- Sing the melody line you hear in your own head. Remember, you don't owe anybody any explanations, you don't owe your parents any explanations, you don't owe your professors any explanations.
  Bono, Commencement Address at the University of Pennsylvania (2004).

- For those who believe, no explanation is necessary; for those who do not believe, no explanation is possible.
  Franz Werfel, The Song of Bernadette (1941, tr. Lewis Lewisohn, 1942).

- I believe that I am not responsible for the meaningfulness or meaninglessness of life, but that I am responsible for what I do with the life I've got.

  Hermann Hesse, Letter (1946, as cited by David Pratt, The Impossible Takes Longer, 2007).

- *DIONYSUS*

  He who believes needs no explanation.

  PENTHEUS

  What's the worth in believing worthless things?

  DIONYSUS

  Much worth, but not worth telling you, it seems.

  Euripides, The Bacchae (406 BC, tr. Colin Teevan, 2002).

- All explanations are against God because explanation de-mystifies existence. Existence is a mystery, and one should accept it as a mystery and not pretend to have any explanation. No, explanation is not needed – only exclamation, a wondering heart, awakened, surprised, feeling the mystery of life each moment.

  Rajneesh, Tao: The Pathless Path (1979).

My faith in you... begins with believing you and believing in who you are, even before I am aware of all you can be. We gradually learn what to believe by knowing first that we believe.

Let go of your mind and then be mindful.
Close your ears and listen!

— *Rumi* [41]

---

[41] See page 95.

8.

Awareness

Faith is awareness based on a spiritual sensuality. It sees what is not otherwise seen and it senses what makes no sense except by the spirit and the experience. Faith is aware of the air one breathes, and being aware it appreciates it, at the top of the mountain and all the way up.

- When the mind is not dissipated upon extraneous things, nor diffused over the world about us through the senses, it withdraws within itself, and of its own accord ascends to the contemplation of God.

  Basil of Caesarea (ca. 379, tr. R. Deferrari, 1926).

- Brethren, we now believe, we do not see; for faith the reward will be to what we believe.

  Augustine of Hippo, Tractates on the Gospel according to John (ca. 420, tr. John Gibb, 1873).

- But when we shall have arrived at that place where we shall reign, no need will there be to say the Creed. We shall see God; God himself will be our vision; the vision of God will be the reward of our present faith.

  Augustine of Hippo, Sermon 8 (ca. 430, tr. R. G. MacMullen, 1844).

- O World, thou choosest not the better
     part!
  It is not wisdom to be only wise,
  And on the inward vision close the eyes,
  But it is wisdom to believe the heart.

  George Santayana, Sonnets and Other Verses (1906).

- Then he said to Thomas, "Put your finger here and see my hands. Reach out your hand and put it in my side. Do not doubt but believe." Thomas answered him, "My Lord and my God!" Jesus said to him, "Have you believed because you have seen me? Blessed are those who have not seen and yet have come to believe."

  Jesus and Thomas (ca. 33; as cited by Anon., John 20:27-29, ca. 100, tr. NRSV, 2021).

- By faith [Moses] left Egypt, unafraid of the king's anger, for he persevered as though he saw him who is invisible.

  Anon., Hebrews 11:27 (ca. 64, tr. NRSV, 2021).

- Faith — is the Pierless Bridge
  Supporting what We see
  Unto the Scene that We do not.

  Emily Dickinson, Faith—is the Pierless Bridge (1865).

- Although you have not seen him, you love him, and even though you do not see him now, you believe in him and rejoice with an indescribable and glorious joy.

  Paul the Apostle, 1 Peter 1:8 (ca. 67, tr. NRSV, 2021).

- Seeing's believing, but feeling's the truth.
  Thomas Fuller, Gnomologia (1732).

- For we walk by faith, not by sight.
    Paul the Apostle, 2 Corinthians 5:7 (ca. 56, tr. NRSV, 2021).

- I cannot look at something through someone else's eyes. I can only truly know something which I know.
    Zhuangh Zhou, The Book of Chuang Tzu (ca. 310 BC, tr. Martin Palmer and Elizabeth Bruilly, 1996).

- We discover sensible things by our senses, rational things by our reason, things intellectual by understanding; but divine and celestial things he has reserved for the exercise of our faith, which is a kind of divine and superior sense in the soul.
    John Bunyan, The Pilgrim's Progress from This World, to That Which Is to Come, The Third Part (ca. 1688).

- When the mind maintains awareness, yet does not mingle with the senses, nor the senses with sense impressions, then self-awareness blossoms.
    Patanjali, Yoga Sutras (ca. 400).

- The Way to see by Faith is to shut the Eye of Reason: The Morning Daylight appears plainer when you put out your Candle.
    Benjamin Franklin, Poor Richard's Almanack (1758).

- Let go of your mind and then be mindful. Close your ears and listen!
  Rumi, Ripened Fruit (ca. 1273, tr. Kamir Helminski and Ahmad Rezwani, 2008).

- Let your eyes look directly forward and your gaze be straight before you.
  Solomon (ca. 931 BC, as cited by Anon., Proverbs 4:25, ca. 400 BC, tr. NRSV, 2021).

- My faith looks up to Thee.
  Ray Palmer, My Faith Looks Up to Thee (1830).

- Sorrow looks back, worry looks around, faith looks up.
  Quentin Edwards (ca. 1995, as cited by Ken Gaub, Sky High Faith, 1995).

- I have been to the mountaintop. ...And I've seen the promised land.
  Martin Luther King Jr., I Have A Dream (1963).

- I lift up my eyes to the hills—from where will my help come? My help comes from the Lord, who made heaven and earth.
  Anon., Psalm 121:1-2 (ca. 979 BC, tr. NRSV, 2021).

- I choose the ascending path because my heart drives me toward it. "Upward! Upward! Upward!" my heart shouts, and I follow it trustingly.

    Nikos Kazantzakis, The Saviors of God: Spiritual Exercises (1960).

- If the doors of perception were cleansed everything would appear to man as it is, infinite.

    William Blake, The Marriage of Heaven and Hell (1793).

- I believe in Christianity as I believe that the Sun has risen, not only because I see it, but because by it I see everything else.

    C. S. Lewis, Is Theology Poetry? (Speech to the The Oxford Socratic Club, 1944)

- Do not complain and cry and pray, but open your eyes and see, for the light is all about you, and it is so wonderful, so beautiful, so far beyond anything of which men have ever dreamt, for which they have ever prayed, and it is for ever and for ever.

    Gautama Buddha (ca. 483 BC, as cited by Charles Webster Leadbeater, The Masters and the Path, 1925).

My faith in you... is my awareness of you, finding you across time and miles, feeling close to you wherever you are. You are not always in my sight, but you are in my heart.

Life... goes on. It always has.
It always will. Don't forget that.
— *Robert Frost* [42]

---

[42] See page 101.

9.

Acceptance

Faith is acceptance without argument, before the challenge and beyond the fight. By acceptance, faith allows the possibility, appreciates the wonder and affirms the awareness. Faith does not pace in the uncertainty of things but stands in awe, eager to understand and accept whatever may come.

- Faith … is the art of holding on to things your reason has once accepted in spite of your changing moods.
  C. S. Lewis, Mere Christianity (1952).

- This being human is a guest house. Every morning a new arrival.

  A joy, a depression, a meanness, some momentary awareness comes as an unexpected visitor.

  Welcome and entertain them all!
  Rumi, The Guest House (ca. 1273, tr. Coleman Barks, 2004).

- For after all, the best thing one can do when it is raining, is to let it rain.
  Henry Wadsworth Longfellow, The Birds of Killingworth (1863).

- All forces have been steadily employ'd to complete and delight me,
  Now on this spot I stand with my robust soul.
  Walt Whitman, Song of Myself (1855).

- Put an end to karma, nurture your awareness, and accept what life brings.
  Bodhidharma, Bloodstream Sermon (ca. 528, tr. Red Pine, 1989}.

- ...And whatever a man knows, whatever is not mere rumbling and roaring that he has heard, can be said in three words.

  > *Ferdinand Kürnberger, Setting Monuments in Opposition (1873, as cited by Ludwig Wittgenstein, Tractatus Logico-Philosophicus, 1922, tr. D. F. Pears and B. F. McGuiness, 1961).*

- In three words I can sum up everything I've learned about life. It goes on. ...It always has. It always will. Don't forget that.

  > *Robert Frost (1954, as cited by Ray Josephs, Robert Frost's Secret (1954, This Week Magazine).*

- The most beautiful thing we can express is the mysterious. It is the source of all true art and science. He to whom this emotion is a stranger, who can no longer pause to wonder and stand rapt in awe is as good as dead; his eyes are closed.

  > *Albert Einstein, What I Believe (1930, Forum and Century).*

- The ultimate gift of conscious life is a sense of the mystery that encompasses it.

  > *Lewis Mumford, The Conduct of Life (1951).*

- There are all kinds of interesting questions that come from a knowledge of science, which only adds to the excitement and mystery and awe of a flower. It only adds. I don't understand how it subtracts.

  Richard Feynman, What Do You Care What Other People Think? (1988).

- Now is it that hardly any major religion has looked at science and concluded, "This is better than we thought! The Universe is much bigger than our prophets said, grander, more subtle, more elegant?" Instead they say, "No, no, no! My god is a little god, and I want him to stay that way." A religion old or new, that stressed the magnificence of the universe as revealed by modern science, might be able to draw forth reserves of reverence and awe hardly tapped by the conventional faiths. Sooner or later, such a religion will emerge.

  Carl Sagan, Pale Blue Dot (1994).

- When we affirm that philosophy begins with wonder, we are affirming in effect that sentiment is prior to reason.

  Richard Weaver, Ideas have Consequences (1948).

- Awe is an intuition for the dignity of all things, a realization that things not only are what they are but also stand, however remotely, for something supreme. Awe is a sense for transcendence, for the reference everywhere to mystery beyond all things. It enables us to perceive in the world intimations of the divine...

  Awe precedes faith; it is the root of faith. We must be guided by awe to be worthy of faith.
  Abraham Joshua Heschel, Who Is Man? (1965).

- The words he uttered shall not pass away;
  For they sank into me - the bounteous
    gift
  Of One whom time and nature had made
    wise,
  ...Of One in whom persuasion and belief
  Had ripened into faith, and faith become
  A passionate intuition...
  William Wordsworth, The Excursion (1814).

- A good man, through obscurest
    aspirations,
  Has still an instinct of the one true way.
  Johann Wolfgang von Goethe, Faust (1808, tr. Bayard Taylor, 1889).

- Moral will plus imagination are the two elements of which faith is compounded. ...The victorious man in the day of crisis is the man who has the serenity to accept what he cannot help and the courage to change what must be altered.
  Reinhold Niebuhr (ca. 1932; as cited by Winnifred Crane Wygal, diary entry, 1932).

- God grant me Serenity to accept the things I cannot change, Courage to change the things I can, and Wisdom to know the difference.
  Reinhold Niebuhr, as cited by Alcoholics Anon., 1940, and, with slight variation, by Winnifred Crane Wygal, We Plan Our Worship Services, 1940).

- The day of my spiritual awakening was the day I saw and knew I saw all things in God and God in all things.
  Mechtild of Magdeburg, The Flowing Light of the Godhead (ca. 1282, tr. Frank Tobin, 1997)

- Faith sees God's face in every human face.
  Catherine Doherty, Poustinia (1975).

- When you see God in everyone, then they see God in you.
  Thomas Merton (ca. 1968; as cited by Raymond Wells, Thomas Merton: In His Own Words, 2021).

My faith in you... accepts you at face value for everything you are: amazing, beautiful, brave and wise as only you can be. And the more I see of you, the more I am in awe of you.

Know why you believe,
understand what you believe,
and possess a reason
for the faith that is in you.
— *Frances Wright* [43]

---

[43] See page 108.

10.

Understanding

Faith is understanding beyond reason, the pursuit of truth that transcends the argument. Faith rises to the occasion of things it cannot comprehend, ready to believe in an answer to what reason asks and knowing there is more to truth than questions can ever grasp.

- Understanding is the reward of faith. Therefore, seek not to understand that thou mayest believe, but believe that thou mayest understand.

  Augustine of Hippo, Tractates on the Gospel of John (ca. 420, tr. John Gibb, 1873).

- I am not going to question your opinions. I am not going to meddle with your belief. I am not going to dictate to you mine. All that I say is, examine; enquire. Look into the nature of things. Search out the ground of your opinions, the for and the against. Know why you believe, understand what you believe, and possess a reason for the faith that is in you.

  Frances Wright, Divisions of Knowledge (1828).

- Since we can never know anything for sure, it is simply not worth searching for certainty; but it is well worth searching for truth.

  Karl Popper, In Search of a Better World (1994).

- And what can be beyond truth except error? So how are you averted?

  Muhammad, Quran 10:32, (ca. 632, tr. Saheeh International, 1997).

- What is truth? said jesting Pilate, but would not stay for an answer.

    Francis Bacon, Of Truth (1625).

- Pilate asked him, "So you are a king?" Jesus answered, "You say that I am a king. For this I was born, and for this I came into the world, to testify to the truth. Everyone who belongs to the truth listens to my voice." Pilate asked him, "What is truth?"

    Jesus and Pontius Pilate (ca. 33; as cited by Anon., John 18:37-38, ca. 100, tr. NRSV, 2021).

- Truth cannot be memorized. Truth has to be discovered now, from moment to moment. It is always fresh, always new, always there for the still, innocent mind.

    Barry Long, Knowing Yourself: The True in the False (1983).

- A very great deal more truth can become known than can be proven.

    Richard Feynman, Nobel Lecture (1965).

- Anyone who claims to know something does not yet have the necessary knowledge.

    Paul the Apostle, 1 Corinthians 8:2 (ca. 54, tr. NRSV, 2021).

- The true value of a man is not determined by his possession, supposed or real, of Truth, but rather by his sincere exertion to get to the Truth. It is not possession of the Truth, but rather the pursuit of Truth by which he extends his powers and in which his ever-growing perfectibility is to be found.

  Gotthold Ephraim Lessing, Anti-Goeze (1778, tr. Scott Horton, Harper's Magazine, 2007).

- Truth draws strength from itself and not from the number of votes in its favor.

  Pope Benedict XVI, Address to the Holy See's International Diplomats (2006, tr. Vatican Publishing House).

- An error does not become truth by reason of multiplied propagation, nor does truth become error because nobody sees it. Truth stands, even if there be no public support. It is self sustained.

  Mahatma Gandhi, Young India (1925).

- I have therefore found it necessary to deny knowledge, in order to make room for faith.

  Immanuel Kant, Critique of Pure Reason, Preface to Second Edition (1787, tr. Norman Kemp Smith, 1929).

- Faith begins precisely where thinking leaves off.

  Søren Kierkegaard, Fear and Trembling (1843, tr. Sylvia Walsh, 2006).

- Truth can be found only through the negation of all thoughts about it.

  Shantha N. Nair, Echoes of Ancient Indian Wisdom (2008, with reference to the "neti-neti" doctrine, Yajnavalkya, Brihadaranyaka Upanishad 2.3.6, ca. 700 BC).

- Now therefore the description: 'Not this, not this.' Because there is no other and more appropriate description than this 'Not this.' Now Its name: 'The Truth of truth.' The vital force is truth, and It is the Truth of that.

  Anon., Brhadaranyaka Upanishad 2.3.6 (ca. 700 BC, tr. Swami Madhavananda, 1950).

- Reason is the greatest enemy that faith has.

  Martin Luther, Table Talk (1569, tr. William Hazlitt, 1872).

- Reason always stands in need of being purified by faith.

  Pope Benedict XVI, Charity in Truth (2009, tr. Vatican Publishing House).

- The last function of reason is to recognize that there are an infinity of things which surpass it.

  Blaise Pascal, Pensées (ca. 1662, published 1670, tr. William Finlayson Trotter, 1931).

- Faith goes before; understanding follows after.

  Augustine of Hippo, Sermons 68 (ca. 430, tr. R. G. MacMullen, 1844).

- Faith therefore has no fear of reason but seeks it out and has trust in it. Just as grace builds on nature and brings it to perfection, so faith builds upon and perfects reason.

  Pope John Paul II, Faith and Reason (1998, tr. Vatican Publishing House).

- The greatest act of faith is when a man understands he is not God.

  Oliver Wendell Holmes Jr., Letter to William James (1907).

- The grateful person knows that God is good, not by hearsay but by experience.

  Thomas Merton, Thoughts in Solitude (1958).

My faith in you... has, beyond my deficiencies, every reason to see you as real and believe that you are true: I want to know you and understand you, and I begin by opening my eyes.

Assurance is glory in the bud,
it is the suburbs of paradise.
— *Thomas Brooks* [44]

---

[44] See page 116.

11.

Assurance

Faith reaches its better part with the blessed assurance of being able to stand at ease, full of both confidence and serenity, knowing what you know with certitude and believing what you believe with all your mind, heart and soul.

- Now faith is the assurance of things hoped for.

    Anon., Hebrews 11:1 (ca. 64, tr. NRSV, 1989).

- Let us approach with a true heart in full assurance of faith.

    Anon., Hebrews 10:22 (ca. 64, tr. NRSV, 2021).

- Assurance is the fruit that grows out of the root of faith.

    Stephen Charnock, Unbelief, The Greatest Sin (ca. 1680).

- Assurance is glory in the bud, it is the suburbs of paradise.

    Thomas Brooks, Heaven on Earth (1657).

- Faith is our seal; assurance of faith is God's seal.

    Christopher Ness, An Antidote Against Arminianism (1847).

- However logical our induction, the end of the thread is fastened upon the assurance of faith.

    Edwin Hubbel Chapin, Characters in the Gospels: Illustrating Phases of Character at the Present Day (1852).

- All men who live with any degree of serenity live by some assurance of grace.
  Reinhold Niebuhr, Reflections at the End of an Era (1934).

- I admire the serene assurance of those who have religious faith. It is wonderful to observe the calm confidence of a Christian with four aces.
  Mark Twain (ca. 1910; as cited by Herbert Moulton, Mark Twain's America, 1981).

- You may loan out your umbrella for twelve months, with the serene confidence which a Christian feels in four aces.
  Mark Twain, Virginia City Territorial Enterprise: Information Wanted, in response to a writer asking about the climate in Nevada (1864).

- There is no such thing as absolute certainty, but there is assurance sufficient for the purposes of human life. We may, and must, assume our opinion to be true for the guidance of our own conduct.
  John Stuart Mill, On Liberty (1859).

- And rest assured, my dear daughters, if you lean with all your weight upon Providence, you will find yourselves well supported.
  Théodore Guérin, Letter to the Sisters at Jasper (1842).

- Remember, if I am stopped, this movement will not stop, because God is with the movement. Go home with this glowing faith and this radiant assurance.
  Martin Luther King Jr., Stride Toward Freedom (1958).

- Blessed assurance, Jesus is mine;
  Oh, what a foretaste of glory divine!

  ...This is my story, this is my song,
  Praising my Savior all the day long.
  Fanny Crosby, Blessed Assurance (1873).

- Blessedness is nothing else but the contentment of spirit, which arises from the intuitive knowledge of God.
  Baruch Spinoza, Ethics (1677, tr. R. H. M. Elwes, 1887).

- Have faith, dear heart; this is the thing that is!
  Emma Lazarus, Assurance (ca. 1887).

- The goal of human nature, of any nature is blessedness. If we do not reach this goal, it is a sign that we are headed in the wrong direction.

  Raimon Pannikar, A Dwelling Place for Wisdom (1991, tr. Annemarie S. Kidder, 1993).

- Blessed are the poor in spirit, for theirs is
      the kingdom of heaven.
  Blessed are those who mourn, for they
      will be comforted.
  Blessed are the meek, for they will inherit
      the earth.
  Blessed are those who hunger and thirst
      for righteousness, for they will be
      filled.
  Blessed are the merciful, for they will
      receive mercy.
  Blessed are the pure in heart, for they will
      see God.
  Blessed are the peacemakers, for they will
      be called children of God.

  Jesus (ca. 33, as cited by Anon., Matthew 5:3-9, ca. 90, tr. NRSV, 2021).

- Blessed are you who are hungry now,
      for you will be filled.
  Blessed are you who weep now, for you
      will laugh.

  Jesus (ca. 33, as cited by Anon., Luke 6:21-22, ca. 120, tr. NRSV, 2021).

- Now as they went on their way, [Jesus] entered a certain village, where a woman named Martha welcomed him. She had a sister named Mary, who sat at the Lord's feet and listened to what he was saying. But Martha was distracted by her many tasks, so she came to him and asked, "Lord, do you not care that my sister has left me to do all the work by myself? Tell her, then, to help me." But the Lord answered her, "Martha, Martha, you are worried and distracted by many things, but few things are needed — indeed, only one. Mary has chosen the better part, which will not be taken away from her."

  Jesus and Martha (ca. 33; as cited by Anon., Luke 10:38-42, ca. 120, tr. NRSV, 2021).

- Faith is a grasping of Almighty power;
  The hand of man laid on the arm of
      God; —
  The grand and blessed hour in which
      the things impossible to me
  Become the possible, O Lord, through
      Thee.

  Anna E. Hamilton, Great Is Thy Faith (ca. 1876, as cited by E. R. Burton & Co., He Giveth Sings, 1892).

- It is certain because it is impossible.

  Tertulian, On the Flesh of Christ (ca. 206, tr. Canon Ernest Evans, 1956).

My faith in you...   is assured of who you are. I accept you as a gift and count you as a blessing. I see in you the grace of the giver, from whom all blessings flow, and on your face the countenance of God.

Faith is the bird that feels the light and sings when the dawn is still dark.

— Rabindranath Tagore [45]

---

[45] See page 124.

12.

Hope

Faith is the heartfelt hope in all there is to come. Intellectual reason spurns the hope, spirit and heart of faith, but faith, having its own reasons why, believes in something greater than the argument.

- Losing your way on a journey is unfortunate. But, losing your reason for the journey is a fate more cruel.

  H. G. Wells, Mr. Britling Sees It Through (1916).

- My Lord God, I have no idea where I am going. I do not see the road ahead of me. I cannot know for certain where it will end. Nor do I really know myself, and the fact that I think that I am following your will does not mean that I am actually doing so. But I believe that the desire to please you does in fact please you. And I hope I have that desire in all that I am doing. I hope that I will never do anything apart from that desire. And I know that if I do this you will lead me by the right road though I may know nothing about it. Therefore will I trust you always though I may seem to be lost and in the shadow of death. I will not fear, for you are ever with me, and you will never leave me to face my perils alone.

  Thomas Merton, Thoughts in Solitude (1956).

- Faith is the bird that feels the light and sings when the dawn is still dark.

  Rabindranath Tagore, Fireflies (1928).

- Below the surface stream,
    shallow and light,
  Of what we say and feel—
    below the stream,
  As light, of what we think we feel,
    there flows
  With noiseless current,
    strong, obscure and deep,
  The central stream of what we
    feel indeed.
  > *Matthew Arnold, St. Paul and Protestantism*
  > *(1870).*

- Through love, through hope, and faith's
    transcendent dower,
  We feel that we are greater than we
    know.
  > *William Wordsworth, The River Duddon*
  > *(1820).*

- The heart has its reasons, which reason does not know. We feel it in a thousand things. ...It is the heart which experiences God, and not the reason. This, then, is faith: God felt by the heart, not by the reason.
  > *Blaise Pascal, Pensées (1660, tr. W. F. Trotter*
  > *1910).*

- Faith is reason grown courageous - reason raised to it highest power, expanded to its widest vision.
  L. P. Jacks, Religious Perplexities (1923).

- A speculative faith consists only in the assent of the understanding, but in a saving faith there is also the consent of the heart.
  Jonathan Edwards, Charity and Its Fruits (1738).

- You ask me how I know he lives.
  He lives within my heart.
  Alfred Ackley, He Lives (1932).

- Faith is at the heart of everything we are and everything we do.
  Albert Pujols, Personal Testimony, Pujols Family Foundation (2014).

- For one believes with the heart and so is justified...
  Paul the Apostle, Romans 10:10 (ca. 57, tr. NRSV, 1989; translation later restated as "For one believes with the heart, leading to righteousness...," NRSV, 2021).

- For through the Spirit, by faith, we eagerly wait for the hope of righteousness.
  Paul the Apostle, Galatians 5:5 (ca. 48, tr. NRSV, 2021).

- First, hope and faith differ in regard to their sources. Faith originates in the understanding, while hope rises in the will.

  Secondly, they differ in regard to their functions. Faith says what is to be done. Faith teaches, describes, directs. Hope exhorts the mind to be strong and courageous.

  Thirdly, they differ in regard to their objectives. Faith concentrates on the truth. Hope looks to the goodness of God.

  Fourthly, they differ in sequence. Faith is the beginning of life before tribulation. (Hebrews 11.) Hope comes later and is born of tribulation. (Romans 5.)

  Fifthly, they differ in regard to their effects. Faith is a judge. It judges errors. Hope is a soldier. It fights against tribulations, the Cross, despondency, despair, and waits for better things to come in the midst of evil.

  Martin Luther, Commentary on the Epistle to the Galatians (1535, tr. Theodore Graebner, 1949).

- Without hope faith cannot endure. On the other hand, hope without faith is blind rashness and arrogance because it lacks knowledge. Before anything else a Christian must have the insight of faith, so that the intellect may know its directions in the day of trouble and the heart may hope for better things. By faith we begin, by hope we continue.

  Martin Luther, Commentary on the Epistle to the Galatians (1535, tr. Theodore Graebner, 1949).

- Faith sets hope on work, hope sets patience on work. Faith says to hope, look for what is promised; hope says to faith, So I do, and will wait for it too.

  John Bunyan, Israel's Hope Encouraged; or, What Hope is, and how distinguished from Faith: With Encouragements for a Hoping People (ca. 1688).

- There is no love without hope, no hope without love, and neither love nor hope without faith.

  Augustine of Hippo, The Enchiridion (ca. 420, tr. J. F. Shaw, 1873).

- If you need something to worship, then worship life — all life, every last crawling bit of it! We're all in this beauty together!

  Frank Herbert, Dune Messiah (1969).

My faith in you... hopes you know without me saying it, but loves to tell you anyway: I believe in who you are and where you are going. I send love to you today and have hope for you tomorrow: now and forever, I will keep this faith in you.

All things can be done
for the one who believes.

— *Jesus* [46]

---

[46] See page 19.

Index

Faith is,
based on belief in things not seen,
acceptance of things not proven and
assurance of things to come,
my complete and appreciating trust
in you.